A Dinner Party
in
the Home Counties

Reshma Ruia

Skylark Publications UK
10 Hillcross Avenue, Morden, Surrey SM4 4EA
www.skylarkpublications.co.uk

First Edition: A Dinner Party in the Home Counties

First published in Great Britain in 2019 by:
Skylark Publications UK
10 Hillcross Avenue
Morden
Surrey SM4 4EA
www.skylarkpublications.co.uk

ISBN 978-0-9560840-6-4

British Library Cataloguing in Publication Data: A CIP record for this book can be obtained from the British Library. Onix codes are available on request.

Designed and typeset by Skylark Publications UK.

Cover design and typesetting by **Yogesh Patel**
The cover art by Yogesh Patel: A party at the House of Commons

Printed and bound in Great Britain and through various channels internationally to be printed locally and distributed

All profits from this book go to Word Masala non-profit projects
Additional donations can be made through the Skylark website.

Word Masala and Skylark Publications UK are Non-Profit Social Enterprises ethically paying all taxes due in the UK.

In memory of my father

Shiv Saigal
At night my father's face
rises in my sleep, like the moon.
He is telling me something.

Acknowledgements

Thanks are due to the editors of the following publications in which some of these poems or versions of these poems have appeared:

Time and Tide Anthology, Funny Pearls, May We Borrow Your Country, Lost Balloon, The Good Journal, Visual Verse, The Quiet Letter, Asia Literary Review, LakeView International and *Saudade.*

All my gratitude to Yogesh Patel for believing in this work and for his enthusiasm for the poetic word. Thanks to Debjani Chatterjee MBE FRSL for her insightful foreword and meticulous feedback, and to Lemn Sissay MBE, Rishi Dastidar and Todd Swift for their kind support.

Finally to Raj, Ravi and Sabrina: Thank you for your support in my journey.

Reshma is a recipient of the 2019 Word Masala Debut Poet Award. Her first novel, *'Something Black in the Lentil Soup'*, was described in the Sunday Times as 'a gem of straight-faced comedy.' Her second novel manuscript, *'A Mouthful of Silence,'* was shortlisted for the 2014 SI Leeds Literary Prize. Reshma's short stories and poems have appeared in various British and International anthologies and magazines and commissioned for Radio. She has a PhD and a Masters in Creative Writing from Manchester University, a Bachelor, and Master's Degree with Distinction from the London School of Economics. She is the co-founder of The Whole Kahani - a writers' collective of British South Asian writers. Born in India, but brought up in Italy, her narrative portrays the inherent preoccupations of those who possess a multiple sense of belonging.

Contents

Beginnings

The Space Between

Endings

Foreword

In recent years, Reshma Ruia's novels and short fiction have established her credentials as an Indian British writer, who explores the themes of belonging and identity against a backdrop of social mores and conventions. As such, I now invite readers to join me in welcoming Ruia's debut poetry volume, *A Dinner Party in the Home Counties*, a collection that continues her exploration with all the robust zeal of an Indian diaspora writer lightly treading multiple cultures.

The issues are contemporary and the language is gritty. With a no-nonsense directness and a flair for narrative, Reshma Ruia presents a host of characters – many flawed and larger than life, but all with distinctive voices. Memorable among them is the assertive Mrs Basu, the 'illegal alien' who remains defiant even as she is deported: 'I have a name!' Mrs Basu shouts. 'I am Kamala Basu, tenth class pass.' ['Mrs Basu Leaves Town']

Then there is Xian Chrysanthemum Xu, whose 'name means freshly cut flowers', but who is casually renamed 'Sally' by an anonymous shop assistant. The latter tells her that she looks like a Sally, and adds: 'Nah, I can't call you Mrs Zoo.' ['In which Mrs Xu Becomes a Sally']

There is also the irreverent patient, 'who was old, black and fat', and who seems to enjoy discomfiting her hapless GP. Shuffling out of his surgery, she can't resist throwing him a challenge: 'Did I tell you I'm lesbian as well? / I bet you got no cure for that.' ['The Patient']

Like a modern-day Jane Austen, the Mancunian author lets us eavesdrop on the conversations of middle England drawing rooms. 'One false move. I will be out of place', declares the narrator of the title poem, 'A Dinner Party in the Home Counties', taking care not to drop her cutlery or her vowels!

This is an energetic book by a writer who deserves to be heard and asks for a centre stage platform: 'I have earned my right to claim this slice of sky as my own. To plant my flag.../ Don't push me to the edges of a faded pink map.' ['A Dinner Party in the Home Counties']

Each reader will decide if Reshma Ruia has 'earned' her right, but I commend Skylark Publications for bringing us her fresh bold voice.

Debjani Chatterjee

Debjani Chatterjee, MBE, FRSL
6th September 2019
Sheffield, UK

Beginnings
Be a beginner every single morning
Meister Eckhart

The Beginning

A man wakes up one morning.
Checks his clock. Only four a.m.
He can't go back to sleep.
His wife lies next to him,
legs bunched up together.
A frown cuts her forehead like a knife.
Her mouth pleated in despair.
In the kitchen, the sink piled high
with unwashed plates and pots.
Children's toys pockmark the floor.
He makes a cup of coffee,
kicks Barbie with his bare toe,
opens the bin, throws the dirty dishes in.
The next minute he is out of the door -
a thief slipping out of his own home,
body flinching in the early-morning cold.
In his pyjamas, he starts his car.
He doesn't get far.
He stays on the driveway
of his two-up two-down.
The engine running.
Cigarette burning in his mouth.
The car radio mute.
He waits
for what he does not yet know.

A Dinner Party in the Home Counties

Being peripheral, I can't offer opinions on climate change,
oil prices, the Brexit crisis.
I am a different breed of fish.
Well-meaning white voices throw questions like bait.
"Did you go for an arranged marriage?"
"Where are you from? Originally?"
One false move. I will be caught in their net.
How pleased they look.
I don't drop my cutlery or my vowels.
BAME? Or is it really BLAME?
I become an acronym in certain rooms.
What I feel, think, or eat can never be marginal.

I choose not to talk of sacred cows. Gurus striking
dog down pose.
I have earned my right to claim this slice of sky as my own.
To plant my flag. Sow my seed.
Don't push me to the edges of a faded pink map.
My face pinned to a rogue's gallery labelled "minority
alternative arts."

In Which Mrs XU Becomes a Sally

Mrs Xu became Sally when she went to the shops.
It was simpler this way.
Newly arrived in a little suburb outside town,
she tried to explain her name, Xian Chrysanthemum
Xu, to the girl at the till,
who wished her good morning.
'I am Xian Chrysanthemum Xu,' she said, her right hand
pressed to her chest. Bowing her head.
The girl at the till screwed up her face. Swilled her name
inside her mouth.
'Nah, I can't call you Mrs Zoo.' She waved away her name.
'I'll call you Sally. You look like a Sally. Good Morning, Sally!'
'My name means freshly cut flowers,' Sally explained.
The girl nodded and said: 'Next Please!'
Mrs Xu went to her home, stripped to her underwear.
Cross-examined herself from toe to teeth
in the bathroom mirror.
She ran her fingers around her face. Pulled her nose.
Slapped her thighs. Pinched her ears straight.
She waved her hand like the English Queen
she'd seen once on TV.
'Hello, Sally!' she said. 'Pleased to meet you.'

1947

The year India gained independence from Britain, and the country became divided into India and Pakistan, with the largest migration of people in modern history.

1947. Say it quickly - it's a number.
Say it slowly - it becomes a code.
Opening doors no one can see.
My father, small as a hummingbird,
sits in his chair,
frail of body and brain.
He's made up of medicines and memory.
There's a train running somewhere behind his eyelids.
He is gambolling through a field of wheat where a pink turbaned
scarecrow stands, arms stretched rigidly.
His father's callused hand letting go of his own.

Is that his mother's voice calling?
Quick! Run! We have to catch the train. She gifts him
a single boiled egg for the journey.
Books, slingshot, the red striped ball by the Tulsi plant
in the courtyard-
he remembers them all.
His grandchildren crowd around him.
The girl is doing a PhD on borders and dividing lines.
Tell me about 1947, Nana, she says, tapping his shoulder,
her laptop buzzing like a bee.
He stirs. He smiles. Scratches his chin.
'My ball. My red striped ball -
I must have left it behind,' he says.

Mrs Basu Leaves Town

Mrs Basu crouches in her seat at the airport gate,
chewing rat-like at the ends of her sari. Bullet voices
ricochet around. She grins.
Confused like a fool. Cameras flash.
A policewoman scowls. Moves closer.
Bare white legs pimpled with cold.
Throw us a crumb of a smile, Mrs Basu thinks.
Her bladder aches. Eyes burn from lack of sleep.
Her village - she never wanted to leave it behind.
A nephew's daft idea to make quick money.
Life-savings gone, in feeding the middleman.
Curled like a foetus sleeping behind the kitchen door.
Minding a stranger's child when she could be home
in the courtyard, oiling her daughter's hair.

Illegal alien to be deported - Section 3(c)
the policewoman snarls.
'I have a name!' Mrs Basu shouts. 'I am Kamala Basu,
tenth class pass.'
Her mouth twists in anger.
She pats her heart. Whispers; 'forget the lost years.
Just be glad.'
Hustled to the back of the waiting plane where
passengers fidget, glower and swear.
Strapped in her seat, Mrs Basu lets out a sigh.
She is going home.

Biography

We are bottles of blood walking down the street.
One gentle push. We spill.
Memories and dreams drip-dripping through tightly closed fists.
Mother, sing me a lullaby. We are bottles of blood
she howls.
My mouth pressed softly against her cheek.
Hold on tight my love, she says.
A gentle nudge is all it'll take.
Away we'll go, spilling and spluttering,
desires and dreams drip-dripping fast
through tightly shut fists.
She flings me high as she sings out loud.
Folds her arms, watching me
as I fall.

Inside Edward Hopper's Diner

Inspired by Edward Hopper's painting NightHawks

A large woman in a city where the women are thin,
wear high heels, have air-brushed skin.
She wears sneakers, lets her hair grow grey.
She has big hips and an E Cup chest.
Her hands flutter
between coffee pots and frying pans.
Chopping. Slicing. Carving. Kneading.
Pancakes and blueberry waffles, stacks of toast,
coffee on the go.
Bellies need feeding.
You could say she has a gift for giving.

Men come to the diner, ease off their jackets,
run their thumbs across the laminated menu.
The food shines in technicolour bliss.
Sitting at the Formica counter,
eyes fixed on the TV screen playing reruns of
Marilyn movies, they give her the chat,
tip her with smiles,
an occasional squeeze en route to the loo,
a slap on her generous behind.
She is their special chica, she'll understand.
Payday will be sometime soon.

A Mediterranean Summer

The first time he touched the sea.
His hand drew back. Frightened. Excited.
His fingers couldn't understand the language
of something so slippery, so shiny, so pure.
Days and nights, he walked barefoot beneath the sun.
At night, head pillowed on sand dunes,
he dreams of rain - a feathered claw stroking his cheek.
The rubber dinghy growls.
He smells petrol fumes. He smells fear.
A hundred bodies pressing near.
Closed fists holding their world tight.
Voices holler. He cowers.
Trailing his fingers in the water…aah!
The wine-dark sea.
He could be Ulysses if he wanted.
Weeping for what's left behind or what lies ahead.

The orange jacket floats, skims the water.
A stray sandal. A puckered blanket.
Postcards from an unfinished voyage.
Tilting beach umbrellas block the view.
Champagne shimmers in the noonday sun.
Well-fed bodies arch their backs,
fiddle with their iPhones and iPads.
The DJ's beat drowns the sighs
of those sinking out of sight.
Platters of oysters lie uneaten.
Models strut, pouting lips, Chanel eyes.
'Darling, it's good to be alive,' smirks the Oligarch to his wife.
It is summer on the Med.

Brexit Blues

They're the have-beens, the never-beens,
wheedling their way in, asylum papers in hand.
Their faces carry the anger of distant lands.
Foreign names. Language like a tug of war,
High-pitched consonants and vowels.
Clothes with a whiff of far-off foods:
Coriander, cumin, Jollof rice.
You half-smile at them in the Aldi aisle.
Them. Shuffling their feet, clumsy in their foreign attire.
What's small and spiteful inside you shouts. Run Back!
You don't want their greed to be a blade against your throat.
You don't want their young men running their fingers
over the breasts of your teenage girls.

Boris buses roam the streets, promising
doom and gloom in Technicolor prose.
He's damn right, you think, ringing the Polish plumber
at midnight.
'The bloody boiler's fucked again!' you shout. 'Get here fast!
I'll pay cash.'

Dick Whittington's London

'One plate chicken tikka.
Poppadums to start with.'
Right away, sir! Any drinks, sir.
His mouth folded like a napkin
in an obedient smile.
Eyes lowered, he bows his head.
Glance drifting for a moment
to the lady's lycra décolleté.
Present the bill, the toothpicks, the mint,
count the cash, curse softly, a measly tip.
The feet move through the jungle roar of
couples playing the mating game.
Families toast anniversaries and birthdays.
Voices tinkle like false coins.
The feet move through dark streets bleeding rain,
past shadows swaying in pub doors.
Voices leap out:
Paki bastard - go bugger off home!
Writing home...*dear mother*...
The email glowing like Whittington's London.
Mention the kind man who invites him home for tea.
Leave out the bit where he unzipped his flies
and begged for a kiss.
Talk of the boss who treats him like a son.
His future is golden. He is flying.

Southall Stories

My son crossed the *kala pani*,
Ate beef, slept with foreign women...
I heard him calling in my sleep.
My sari wrapped tight,
I leapt across the *kala pani*,
It was hard at first I will not lie.
The language: an alphabet soup
bubbling inside my mouth.
The grey days shut me in like a wall.
I learnt damn fast: to stop waiting
for the street vendor's call,
to leave my gold bangles behind
when I caught the 151 bus to Asda.
I love the rain that falls all day-every day.
Twenty-four-hour monsoon on tap.
Diwali comes, goes; Holi comes, goes.
No one cares - not even me.
At Christmas, I insist we get a tree.
The English are organised. Very up-to-date.
My son tells me every day.
No dripping roof, no leaking tap.
No wildflowers, no untidy trees.
No unnecessary smiles, no hugs.
Everything trimmed and to the point.
What's not to love?
He gets up for work when the world is asleep.
An MBA at home, he drives DHL vans for a living,
scowls when I watch my Indian TV.
Learn English, Ma, he pleads.
It's time I found a wife for my son.
A girl from back home, plump cheeks, fair skin.
Together we will sit and enjoy BBC.
Kala Paani in Hindu tradition refers to crossing the seas to foreign lands

23

Egg

I hear you at night.
A single cell, you keep sucking
my insides noisily. A parasite
slurping your way through.
Now a limb, an eye, a throat.
You're a dead weight, not a crown.
Don't ask me to shut my eyes and breathe
your name loud like a hymn.
It's too early to be in love with
this accident of cells blurring the ultrasound.
There are no grudges against you. Not yet.
Only this need persists to make you understand.
This blood will still roar though now it whimpers low.
You won't fell me down, my unborn child,
with your love or your blows.

The Space Between
"I'm not as alive as I used to be, but I'm not yet dead. I'm sort of...in-between"
Mitch Albom, *Tuesdays with Morrie*

A Love Story

To Bangkok and Pattaya the old men come.
In neon-lit cocktail bars with come-hither pouts.
Flamingo patterned shirts.
Her Majesty's passport – a calling card.
They barter varicose-veins and beer-stink breath
for caresses and saccharine sighs.
There he stands – Martin, Paul, John and Ian.
Formerly of Doncaster, Crouch End and Nuneaton.
Bending expectant over his gin and lime.
Bright-splashed shorts holding afloat sun-freckled tyres of flesh.

A hero he is – this Martin, Paul, John and Ian.
Fleeing pinstriped and boiler suits.
Fast food counters. Armpit odours on rush-hour tubes.
Kids all grown up. Gone. Wife addicted to sleeping pills and
'Corrie'.

And she - tight ass in a metallic mini skirt.
Nameless. Maybe he'll call her Dolly.
Black hair and child-like limbs.
His everyday-suddenly-becomes-special heroine.
Dead eyes and a ready smile. Fleeing the nightly call centre shift.
The bloated tug of boiled rice in the belly.
The one-roomed tenement she shares with many.
Leaning pensive against posters of American hunks,
she dreams. Young firm men with blond-haired arms.

A room will do. A mattress will do. The naked bulb over a dark
doorway will do. His hands are mice on her skin.
The taste of his beer inside her throat.

Together they come. Hero and heroine
pantomiming a Hollywood kind of love.
One day. Someday soon he'll take her to the beach.
Buy her a mojito. Show her a ring.

The Ballad of an Unfinished Accountant

He wakes up every morning to a grey-black world.
A matchstick figure in a Lowry painting.
Sucked clean of breath and bone, he feels
made up of recollections - of her - of them.
The empty pillow by his side carries the grease
of her absent head. She has been and gone.

He has already built a life with her.
The wedding altar, the kids, summer holidays on the beach.
A mistake he keeps on repeating
with every one-night stand he picks up.
You have a homesick heart, they sigh,
cupping his bald head in their hands. Stroking
his face where wrinkles run deep.
With absent-minded fingers and upset voices,
they plead:
This is a business transaction Mister don't anchor your heart in us.
His heart. He sees it like a balloon - untethered, unmoored,
aimless.
He runs after it - outstretched arms and weeping skin.
He skips, trips, falls, chases his heart as it floats out of view.
Pinning it to the breast of the girl sleeping by his side.
A celebratory rosette.

The alarm clock shrills into life. He dresses in a hurry.
Reports for work in the accountancy firm
where he spends his days filing tax returns
for sad-eyed divorcees and medium-sized companies
planning Brexit.

Pomology

Being a woman can be fun at times.
To be called a shape - a pear or a plum.
A fruit salad deconstructed daily.
Your breasts are ripe mangoes.
Your hips have a melon's flair.
Your mouth - a strawberry ripe for the picking.
A lifelong lesson in pomology it is.
To be classified by the shape of your limbs.
Being a woman is fun up to a point.

One day it's over.
The harvest is ripe, ready to rot.
In your sleep, while you're not watching,
the seed goes sour, the juice runs dry.

No glances. No whistles. All funeral quiet.
You tiptoe down the street.
You still have your fruit.
But it's no longer the season.

New Me: Mother Me

I woke up this morning and turned into my mother.
Rushing to the toilet for a pee,
I grabbed the mirror to my face.
Something went wrong. Something went right.
The face staring back didn't feel like mine.
I slipped on my skirt. Pulled up my tights.
Checked the mirror again. The chin hair.
The sunken eyes, they were hers all right.
My mother's grudges. Her slights.
A lifetime's plunder by my bedside.
I swoop them. I hug them tight.
Limp through my day with a jagged smile.
A heart clenched like a boxer's fist.

Class Reunion

My friend and I are together for tea at last:
Prosecco for her, English Breakfast for me.
Swapping memories.
She begins. I lower my head.
Stare at the teacup's chipped rim.
The brown liquid brews up a storm.
Her words - dead clay birds of dead-end times.
I remember broken fences and walls.
She builds castles of sugar icing and blue lakes.
I whimper of darkness and being summer blind.
She glares at me.
Pea-brain! How can you say such things? She growls.
A most wonderful childhood we had.
The fairy tales she sings to herself.
I forgive them all.

Her rose-tinted yesterdays that she ruled
like a queen have no echo in what she is today.
A woman greedy for a gilded past,
dancing in a room full of trick mirrors
that only know how to lie.

The Patient

I once examined a woman who was old, black and fat.
I asked, Madam *how is your life?*
'Life!' she snorted. 'Can't you see I'm black?'
I moved the papers on my desk and said, *So, what?*
'Try wearing my skin and walking around; you'll soon
see what I mean.'
What else may be wrong? I have my notepad out.
'I'm fat - people see my shape before they see me.'
I look at my watch. She's holding up the queue.
Anything else? One must be patient with the old.
'I'm old. That's what's wrong.
I fumble, fall, dribble and droop.
At night I keep the lights on because I'm afraid of dying.'
I prescribe her anxiety pills: Celexa, Lexapro, Prozac.
A bottle of red wine too.
Strictly for medicinal purposes, I say, my mouth a
smiling line.
She sure has her work cut out.
'Thank you, Doctor.
You're so kind, giving me your time,' she replied.
Shuffling to the door, she turned to look.
'Did I tell you I'm lesbian as well?
I bet you got no cure for that!'

This Could Only Be Lennon's Doing

Imagine a day like no other.
The sky - a blue-skinned Krishna's belly.
Sun dripping its honey.
Widows, clutching walking sticks,
dance can-can on the streets,
hospitals serve truffle meals,
teenagers hunched over Instagram profiles
chuck away their mobiles,
journalists twiddle their thumbs,
dentists drill their own gums.
There is talk of love, not cybercrime.
The airwaves jam. Husbands call wives.
Even the Queen comes down for a pint.
Overhead the planes pin violet hearts to the clouds.

The rich fling open their doors. The refugees arrive
bearing cashew nuts and smiles.
Handshakes and hugs everywhere.
Only the old look wise, unperturbed.
This could only be John Lennon's doing.

El Kapitano

Don't speak of falling in love
as though it were a boulder
you tripped over, stumbled, fell into
the gaping ditch beneath.
You were always clumsy in your body
and in your words.
Speak, instead of climbing into love.
A deliberate act you initiate with alert eyes
and knowing hands. Placing your bare feet:
no crampons, no harness.
Your fingers are bloodied. Your hold is tight.
The red flag of your heart waiting to unfurl
when your upturned face touches the sky.

It Is a Poet's Fault

"He took her for granted, of course he did, but he took her for granted -
not like an old coat in the corner of a dark cupboard, as she'd put it to
herself, but like the very air that he breathed."
- Ahdaf Soueif, *In the Eye of the Sun*

The start was simple.
You quoted these lines.
A dinner party. A school gate. Maybe a high street.
You came up.
A lopsided smile.
A cappuccino in a café
sprinkled with a chocolate heart.
You always insisted on paying.
You had: understanding eyes,
patient hands, plenty of time.

I stripped, giddy like a new-born teenager
in a hurry. Skin to the bone
till I didn't know where your breath began
and mine ended.
One day you remembered who you were:
Your bouquet of words wilted dry,
your eyes threw down shutters,
your wedding band appeared, glinting gold.
You said it was the poet's fault.
Gently, so gently,
your hands pushed me back into the world.

The Dwarf in the Mirror

Consider the dwarf in your mirror.
The one you high-five every morning,
brushing your teeth, checking your gums,
slapping your cheek to bloom some colour.
There is nothing heroic in the smile.
No seed that fruits within the womb.
Just the dull tick-tock of the sun and moon.
Promising death and disease.
Every morning dress this dwarf.
Smack its lips wet. Perfume its belly sweet.
Gargle its mouth with sugar and honey.
String its rosary of words. Trim its gestures.
Then let it loose upon the world.

Monologue of a Priest

The temple squats beneath the sun.
An ancient toad upon the hill.
The clay Gods watch.
Flies play hide and seek among their tattered robes.
The priest waits. Folded hands.
Bowed head. Grasping eyes.
There is a parade of gods in my domain,
he chants: Vishnu, Shiva, Kali and Ganesh.
I have borrowed Shiva's third eye
to stage the pantomime of birth and death.
I watch the pilgrims as they arrive.
Breath suspended. Bewildered gaze.
Cravings of the flesh tucked out of sight.
With the stale scent of bhajans memorised.
My belly jiggling with laughter,
I will hum-haw and ring the temple bells.
Yes, that's right, you will conceive a son
the next full moon. Crack a coconut every noon.
Your daughter will be married
before the harvest is due.
Just cross my palm with a gold coin or two.
I watch as you scuttle away.
Broken-winged birds given the gift of flight.
Congratulating yourselves on bribing the gods
with a kilo of laddus, a fistful of marigold flowers.

The Oligarch and His Muse

Your Lego bricks of cars and homes,
corporate art, off-shore whores.
The shrill whistle you blow.
The world marching to your tune.
Stop hiding behind tinted windows and wings
that whisk you away from factories spewing filth.

Take off your shoes. Your suit of gold.
Leave your Rolex at the door.
Run to me with the clumsy joy
of a new-born babe taking his first step.

The Lord's Prayer

After Brecht's Simple Pleasures

Lord, grant me the quiet perfection
of imperfect days.
The radiator breaking,
the kettle that won't sing,
the train leaving the platform just as I reach.
Lord, grant me sorrows that can be stilled
with toast and tea.
The sound of rain, washing a windowpane.
The world has had enough
of bullets and leaders barking blood,
women clutching babies as they sink.
The world has had enough of peacocks.
Let the sparrows come out to preen.

Endings

But each ending goes on and on
Marianne Boruch, 'Human Atlas'.

A Mrs Dalloway Kind of Day

It was a Mrs Dalloway kind of day.
Nose buried in a bouquet of flowers,
Clarissa strides through the park where
a young man sits, scratching his head.
A swift glance at his hollowed cheeks and she's on her way.
The distant hum of traffic. A bee's roar in her ear.
Easy enough to be happy.
Toss a coin. Swipe a card. Buy the dress. The shoes. The jewels.
Clap away spider webs lurking inside rooms.
The hurt, the bruise, the dripping faucet of an eye.
They belonged to someone else's life.
If only she could run, back to her ten-year-old self
chasing butterflies on the village green.
Cheeks freckled with sunshine, not age.
A heart somersaulting in joy.
Limbs dripping youth.

'Richard will be home soon,' Clarissa thinks,
quickening her step. She browses. She beams.
The shop windows throw back her face.
It feels like applause.
Another candle, bottles of wine, fruit that's in season.
Perhaps quince.
Her life runs through her like a ticker tape.
Peter's face looming close.
His fingers, they were always round and rough, but
soft like winter light on her breast.
A doorbell rings. Footsteps move close.
Mrs Dalloway's party is about to begin.

An Empty Milk Bottle

The hours. The empty hours come rushing in.
The children grown up and gone,
feathering their own nests.
The husband, hiding out of reach,
tripping over his own shadow.
She looks at her hands
sleeping in her lap
and can't quite understand
how and why a life crammed
so full of living and loving
became so stripped. So bereft of meaning.
An empty milk bottle,
idling on the doorstep.

One Day It Is over

There are lives, and lives circling out of reach.
Dancing away, leaving empty rooms behind.
My body throws its arms around every friendly voice it meets.
This need to be understood.
This need to belong.
Who will step forward and fill with sound
the silence in this four-chambered heart?
Who will step forward and break the hands
of the Grandfather clock spinning on my face?
One day it's over.
Glances no longer scissor you on the street.
Rivers no longer part to give you right of way.
Even the hunch-backed builder on the street forgets to whistle
and shout.
Your bones ache. Your chin grows double.
Your bladder leaks at every sneeze.
Your mind is a beehive of muddled voices.
The upward Nike flick of the day
turns into a final downward droop.

A Conversation with Sylvia Plath

Her grave sulks on an ugly slope.
An untidy patch. There are brambles, dandelions too.
A foxglove peeps its head through
the granite slab with its puckered ridges.
Waves in slow motion.
It's a shrine of sorts – this otherworld – for
passing poets and women who carry a carnival of
chaos in their hearts and wombs.
Paper roses. A postcard. A child's rattle rusty gold.
A wedding ring. A photo of a smiling Ted, his face
buried in the nest of her bouncy gold hair
where a red ribbon blooms. A drop of blood.
I lurk there with my empty hands.
I have nothing to give.
She will speak soon.
The clouds bleat heavy with rain.
The church is a clown's face streaked with tears.
Still, I wait.
The trick, she tells me, is to balance while falling.
To stand still while burning quick.

The Pilot

In memory of flight MH-370

The cockpit dashboard blinks
a thousand bleary eyes.
Each dial a finger
spinning him someplace
beyond the star-rimmed sky.
His head in a twist,
which way should he turn?
The continents whirl a dervish dance
around him.
The engine's roar becomes
a soft insect bite on his ear.
He slips his hand inside his pocket,
pulls out a feather, grey-blue,
tender like a baby's early morning breath.
He presses the feather against his cheek.
The day comes back.
The wounded bird from a long-ago childhood.
He knelt by the roadside, knees powdered in the dust,
deaf to his mother's impatient tugging hand.
Carefully he plucked the single drooping feather.
His stare never leaving the bird's stone-hard eye
that was predicting his death.

An Old Man's Mouth

Today you kissed me with an old man's mouth.
Dry lips puckered against my cheek.
The grey stubble of your chin bruising mine.
Your hand fumbled and felt beneath the bedsheet.
You heaved your body over mine.
Pinning me down:
Arms spread-eagled, crucified,
I lay still. My inside's shutting down:
the breast, the liver, the heart.
The jutting hipbone sighs to a stop.
Your rasping breath turns feverish and hot.
I quietly slip away.

The President Is Coming Home

The President's heart is failing. He has spent months
nurturing this pain.
'But there are orders to be signed and laws to be
passed.' The Ministers point to the dusty files on his ivory desk.
The President shakes his head, hands rubbing his chest.
'There is a crack here that won't heal,' he says.
The Ministers fear a coup. Telephone calls are made.
Faxes sent in the hush of night. A fleet of silver-haired doctors
arrives, armed with stethoscopes and sugar-coated pills.
They poke and prod but can't find the root.
'No tumour, no abscess, no perforated lung or limb,' they say, as
they tot up their bill
The President offers them rooibos tea, cardamom
macaroons, platters of plantain chips.
At daybreak, he has them lined outside the palace
walls. Dispatched to heaven with a single gunshot.
The pain persists. A lover's kiss, it feeds on his skin.
One night a young man appears in his dream. He says:
'Go back to your village and become one with your
people'. It's Jesus, showing him the way.

The President's Rolls glides towards his ancestral
village, past ochre anthills and bare fields.
The President sits. Goose feather pillows cushion his back,

a rosary of pearls dangles from his wrist,
his index finger rests on a page of King James' Bible.
Eyes, sunk within their folds of fat weep.
In the village, the men rush to button their rags.
The women sweep their huts clean.
Empty-bellied dogs, the old and the sick kicked out of sight.
They wait with folded hands and toes curled in fright.
The President steps out and kneels,

forehead pressed to the ground.

Slowly he strips, discarding his Saville Row suiting,
shoes handmade in Italy, jewels to make the sun blink.
Naked he stands before his people,
hands cupped like a begging bowl.
'I have come to mend my heart. To be one with you,' he says.
'We want our President back with his diamonds and
his robes,' the villagers hiss and yell. They gather their sticks
and shoo him away.
He runs, trips and falls. His heart leaping out through a crack.
'Aaaahh,' the President sighs, holding his heart in his fist like a
rose. Peace. At last!

A Goodbye

An April afternoon.
The sad hulking shape of her father in the window.
Her mother limping up the steps,
one hand raised.
The torrent of her words bruising her ear.
Make something of your life
Before it's too late.
The yellow cab in the driveway.
The bonnet splattered with fallen cherry blossoms.
Another goodbye. Another flight home.
'I'll be back soon,' she promises,
flying back towards her other life.

Made Helpless by Age

We wait our turn
Lot's wife. Afraid
to take a last look.
Snake-thin waist, dewy eyes,
American white teeth.
We've traded in our lost selves
for chipped nails and sagging breasts.
An exhale of breath. A sharp intake.
A gasp. A wheeze.
Before we know it
We've run out of time.

For Better, for Worse

My husband has quiet, capable, doctor-hands.
We live alone, contented.
In a little house in a little suburb in a little town.
We prune our dahlias in time, wave to the neighbours,
every September take a cruise down the Rhine.
The drive to the hospital takes my husband ten minutes.
My work as a librarian is a half-hour commute.
One day my husband forgets to come home.
He sits crouching on the hard shoulder of the M56.
His car purrs beside him like a pet cat.
He is naked. His clothes lie next to him in a neat pile.
Tea-brown skin goose-bumped in cold. He keeps his glasses on.
The police are kind. They hand him a blanket,
swaddle him like a baby and bring him home to me.
My husband leans against the window,
the Sudoku unfinished on his lap.
His eyes are milky blue with fright.
His mouth dribbles. He calls me names at night:
'Bitch. Whore. Prostitute.'
In the morning, I feed him milk and porridge.
Line his pills; pretend they're jelly babies on the plate,
wash his face, wipe his bum.
Keep his chicken nuggets ready for the microwave.
I shut the door softly, so he won't hear me leave.
In the library, I exchange a joke or two about the grey
English summer.
Spend my lunchtime reading Emily Dickenson.

I Will Be Home for Tea

In memory of Yousef Makki

'I will be home for tea,' he phones his mum
that afternoon, walking on the tree-lined avenue.
The big houses. The gardens. The fancy cars.
He sees them all. He wants them all.
Spring is around the corner. His school had said.
Burnage didn't matter, he was Oxbridge bound. He'd go far.
Round the bend, the big boys come.
Racing on their bikes, a glint of mischief in their eyes,
a glint of steel in their jean pockets.
They circle him.
'Yo, bro? You up for it?' Old scores need settling fast.

All of it - the houses, the cars, the flower-crowded gardens.
The mum waiting by the door, mobile held to her ear.
A by-line in the local north-west news.

Tell Me About Old Age

The child asks his grandmother.
All day you sit, moan and count your pills.
Call your kids. Grumble about bills.
You do nothing. Doesn't seem like much fun to me, he says.
They sit in the garden.
The child at the woman's feet.
It's summer. The heat is like a boiled sweet
stuck inside his cheek but grandma's shoulders wear
a thick alpaca shawl, like a witch's cape.
There are striped red socks on her feet.
Grandma shuts her eyes and thinks.
The shrill telephone bell of memory never stops.
'Being old is a full-time job.' She winks.

Portrait of a Family

No one rings my father. He meets no one for coffee.
He plays no golf, no poker. There are no girlie magazines
in his loo.
Dinner times he sits across us. His face a foreign map.
He pats our heads with affection.
His kind words float around us, soap bubbles
with no weight. Always considerate, always polite,
he tiptoes around our lives.
His love is like a handshake from a retiring
well-meaning colleague.
My mother is different.
Her worries stalk our sleep.

She was beautiful until we arrived.
Then she became an archaeological site plundered bare.
Our little heads and hearts clamouring for care.
Her mind, once a galloping horse,
now frets in front of daytime soaps.
She sometimes forgets to brush her hair,
drinks PG Tips to pass time, eats cakes for comfort,
cuts out discount vouchers for Caribbean cruises she'll never take.
Two deep lines run down the sides of her nose
like a railway track.
Only her love for us burns bright.
A large open flame drip-dripping blood.

Van Gogh's Bed

Saint-Paul Asylum, Saint-Rémy

The irises have gone.
Blue petals ripped by the mistral.
Swept over the vineyards.
The golden blur of the rolling fields.
The lavender is also gone.
Dry stalks like origami, the shade of Parker ink.
Inside your room tourists pause,
mobiles in hand.
This is no time for selfies or dinner plans.
They circle your bed, saucer-eyed in disbelief.
'To think his paintings go for a million bucks!'
The stage whispers are loud.
Don't let them disturb your sleep.
Your bed is a pauper's bed-sagging mattress.
Rusty metal frame, too narrow and small
for your thrashing limbs.
And your big head - a honeycomb of bones and headaches
and visions too.
Swirly trees, shooting stars, the purple mole
on a young woman's clavicle.
You prefer to keep them to yourself.
You lay this head down each night,
turning towards the square window
through which flutters
the cobalt handkerchief of the sky.

Overheard at Cindy Sherman's Show at the National Gallery

The bold mouth that sneers. The curled eyelash.
The body gift-wrapped in feather and flounce,
demanding your gaze.
Cindy hangs on the walls, bouncing from Beverly Hills
to Cape Cod. Donning disguises that titillate the senses:
Madonna, Monroe, cocktail waitresses and bored
housewives - she's been them all.
She's a chronicler of a gilded age.
But, you're not listening.
You wear sensible flat sandals and short grey hair.
Your lips have not kissed a lipstick in a hundred years.

You're talking – loud and urgent. Fish words swim out of
your mouth, gasping for oxygen.
The museum guard raises an eyebrow, buries a yawn,
shifts one buttock cheek, then the other on the folding metal stool.
You are two kind old ladies of late middle age. He won't
disturb you. He'll let it pass.
This is what you have to say:
Brother Richard is still being a dick. He forgot to ring Mother on
Mother's Day. Sister Margaret has hit the bottle again. What about your
allotment? Did you catch the thieves? Who would've thought courgettes
were so prized! Not courgettes? Sorry, did you say runner beans? My
hearing is not what it used to be. You got the smear test back? Yes, my
knees are playing up again. That homeopathy woman you suggested, I
think she's a quack. Three pounds fifty they charged for a measly cup of
coffee in the café upstairs! What did I tell you? Greggs would've been
better. I worry about Paul most days. The other day he left the crossword
unfinished. Again! Most unlike him, and yes, did you visit the grave?
Can't believe he's been ten years gone? And the kids? And the kids?
Mark's planning on emigrating to Australia. You mean immigrating?
No, I meant emigrating. It's what rich folks do when they set up home in
another country. This country is going to the dogs. Just look at that
guard, lazy sod, not doing his job!

Soft Peaches

They are soft peaches left in the sun too long.
They bruise easily.
Their milk teeth grow old within their cheeks,
fall by the roadside. Become dentures.
Their heart is an umbrella stand
on which they hang rosaries of
petty disappointments and dreads.
Medical prescriptions and utility bills.
Death is a salesman who rings every night,
keeping them awake.

Chesapeake Bay

On laying my father to rest

I learnt something new today. Ash is not ash.
It is pulverized bone ground to dust.
Walking the summer happy streets of Annapolis.
Navy cadets all starched white uniform and smiling teeth.
And you, poured into a plastic pouch, swinging from my shoulder
inside a Wholefoods jute bag. Light. Bird-light you are snug
against my hip.
Even in death, attentive and polite.
The Chesapeake Bay it had to be.
No temple-strewn Ghats of Haridwar where pundits sit and scowl,
salivating like dogs
promising reincarnation for a gold coin.
We're selfish. We want you close. Beneath the unending
prairie of this American sky.
How proud you were, repeating the oath to the stars and stripes.
George Bush beckoning you to the land of the free and bold.
Afterwards, we celebrated with a sandwich and caffeine-free Coke.

I wade in. Chesapeake Bay - a kiss curl around my knees.
Clumsy, I bow and scoop you out: dull grains, no glint of gilt, you
pucker in my palm.
My knuckles spread you out like basting butter on the water's skin.
An atom of liquid and light you linger on, clinging to my
fingertips, a life raft.
You never learnt to swim.

There are roses, guiltily plucked from a stranger's garden.
Some Ganges water in a plastic bottle. Cow's milk too.
I mix them all, an unholy mess staining the water.
Back on the beach, the IPhone bursts into song.
Devotional, trite, the high-pitched voice
calling on Gods to bid you adieu.
You would have preferred Sinatra and a slice of pepperoni pizza
for your final send-off.

Recent books by Skylark Publications UK

Swimming with Whales *by Yogesh Patel* ISBN 9780956084057
A Certain Way *by Mona Dash* ISBN 9780956084040
Word Masala Award Winners 2015   ISBN 9780956084033
Word Masala 2011 ISBN 9780956084019
Bottled Ganges *by Yogesh Patel* ISBN 9780956084002

Please visit: http://www.skylarkpublications.co.uk/bookshop.html

*

Word Masala Foundation

The foundation promotes South-Asian diaspora poets and writers by awarding them for their excellence in poetry.

Instead of a monetary prize, it helps them by working as a non-commercial agent, by organising reviews, highlighting their work in publications and magazines, organising readings and events, and placing articles and interviews where possible.

The foundation is a non-commercial thrust and believes very strongly in working with other likeminded stakeholders. It also awards them with a recognition plaque highlighting their efforts in diversity. Hence, our work is far from done. We can be consulted on improving the diversity in your programme. Do contact us if you are as passionate as we are about the equal opportunity for all.

Yogesh Patel, poet, publisher and the founder
Lord Bhikhu Parekh, Patron
Lord Navnit Dholakia, Patron